TARANTULAS

by Jaclyn Jaycox

PEBBLE
a capstone imprint

Pebble Explore is published by Pebble, an imprint of Capstone.
1710 Roe Crest Drive
North Mankato, Minnesota 56003
www.capstonepub.com

Library of Congress Cataloging-in-Publication Data is available on the Library of Congress website.
ISBN: 978-1-9771-1346-7 (library binding)
ISBN: 978-1-9771-1799-1 (paperback)
ISBN: 978-1-9771-1354-2 (eBook PDF)

Summary: Simple text and photographs present tarantulas, their body parts, and behavior.

Photo Credits
Alamy: BIOSPHOTO, 22; Newscom: Andrea & Antonella Ferrari/NHPA/Photoshot, 27; Science Source: Kenneth M. Highfill, 23; Shutterstock: Allmy, 12, asawinimages, 17, bchyla, 7, Cathy Keifer, 21, 24, Dan Olsen, 11, Milan Zygmunt, Cover, 18, Nenad Nedomacki, 16, R McPherson, 26, Ryan M. Bolton, 14, Safwan Abd Rahman, 19, socool23, 5, Vaclav Sebek, 1, wawritto, 9, wolfness72, 13, xtotha, 8, 15

Editorial Credits
Hank Musolf, editor; Dina Her, designer; Morgan Walters, media researcher; Tori Abraham, production specialist

All internet sites appearing in back matter were available and accurate when this book was sent to press.

Printed and bound in China.
002489

Table of Contents

Words in **bold** are in the glossary.

Amazing Tarantulas

Many people are afraid of spiders, especially big, hairy ones! Tarantulas are not a danger to people. They are calm animals. They won't attack unless threatened. Some people even keep them as pets.

Tarantulas are a type of **arachnid**. There are about 900 kinds. They are the biggest spiders in the world.

Where in the World

Tarantulas live on every **continent** except Antarctica. Most live in South America. They also live in the United States, Mexico, Australia, southern Asia, and Africa.

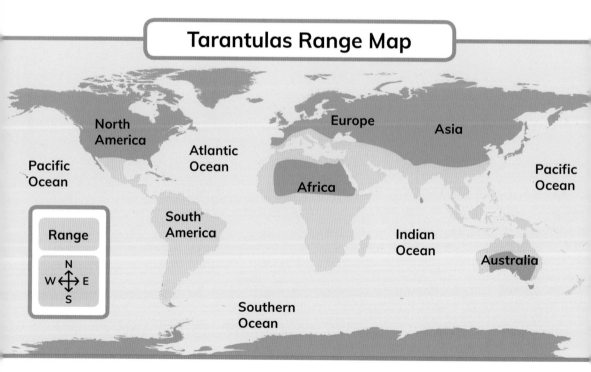

Tarantulas Range Map

North America

Europe

Asia

Pacific Ocean

Atlantic Ocean

Africa

Pacific Ocean

Range

N
W E
S

South America

Indian Ocean

Australia

Southern Ocean

Tarantulas live in warm **habitats**. They can be found in jungles. These hot places have many plants. They can also be found in dry deserts.

Tarantulas live in different places. Most live in **burrows** underground. They dig these holes with their fangs and legs. They put silk on their walls. This keeps dirt from falling in. They can climb in the hole. They can climb out too.

Other types live under rocks. Some live under logs. Some even live high in trees.

Big, Hairy Spiders

Tarantulas come in different sizes. Some have legs that stretch across 5 inches (12.7 centimeters). Others stretch across 11 inches (28 cm). The smallest weigh about 0.9 ounces (25.5 grams). The biggest can weigh more than 3.5 ounces (99 g).

Tarantulas have different colors too. Many are brown or black. Some are blue or pink. They can also have stripes or spots.

Tarantulas have eight legs. They have eight eyes. Their hair makes them different from other spiders. It covers their bodies and legs. The hair helps them climb.

The hair also protects them from **predators**. These animals hunt spiders. A tarantula is ready if an animal attacks. It can flick hairs at the attacker. The hair can hurt the attacker's eyes. It gives the spider time to escape. Zoom!

On the Menu

A tarantula waits in its burrow. It's dark out. It knows a bug is walking by. The tarantula jumps on it. It bites the bug. It waits for it to stop moving. Dinner time!

Other spiders use webs to catch food. Tarantulas don't use webs. But some leave a line of silk outside their burrows. When **prey** touches it, the tarantula knows food is there.

Tarantulas hunt at night. They can't see well. Instead they sense small back-and-forth movements. They sense these **vibrations** with their legs. They can also use their hairs. This helps tarantulas know what is close.

Tarantulas have strong jaws. When they bite their prey, their fangs let out **venom**. The venom kills their prey. Tarantulas can't eat solid food. They have to turn their prey into liquid. Tarantulas use their straw-like mouths to suck up the animals. Slurp!

fangs

Tarantulas eat many kinds of animals. Most tarantulas eat bugs. They also eat other spiders and small lizards. They eat mice, snakes, and frogs too. Some tarantulas even eat birds. Tarantulas can go days without food. They often have big meals. They can wait a month between eating.

Tarantulas also drink water. They find drops of water on leaves, or on puddles on the ground.

Life of a Tarantula

Tarantulas spend most of their time at home. They live alone. They only come together to **mate**. A male leaves his burrow to find a female. He builds a web. He dances to attract the females. The males leave after mating. They can't stay too long. The females might try to eat them!

A female lays between 50 and 2,000 eggs. She wraps them in silk. This keeps them safe. After six to nine weeks, the eggs hatch.

Baby tarantulas are called spiderlings. Newborns are less than 0.2 inches (0.5 centimeters) wide. That is half the size of a pea! After hatching, they leave the burrow to live on their own.

old skin

tarantula after molting

Tarantulas have to **molt** in order to grow. They wiggle out of their old skin. They leave the old skin behind. Young spiderlings molt about once a month. Tarantulas molt until they are 7 or 8 years old.

Tarantulas don't only molt to grow. If a leg is lost, it will regrow while molting.

Males can live up to 7 years. Most die not long after mating. Female tarantulas live longer than males. They can live up to 30 years in the wild.

Dangers to Tarantulas

Few animals eat tarantulas in the wild. Birds, large lizards, and snakes sometimes eat them.

Tarantula hawks are the biggest danger. These are large wasps. They sting tarantulas. Then they lay their eggs on the spiders. When the eggs hatch, the developing wasps eat the tarantulas.

Habitat loss is a danger to some tarantulas. Trees can get cut down. The tarantulas that live there lose their homes. People also keep tarantulas as pets. But too many are being taken out of their homes to be used as pets. Some kinds of tarantulas are in danger. They are at risk of dying out. Laws are put into place to protect them.

Fast Facts

Name: tarantula

Habitat: deserts, jungles, rain forests

Where in the World: found on every continent except Antarctica

Food: bugs, spiders, mice, toads, snakes, small lizards, birds

Predators: tarantula hawks, birds, large snakes, and lizards

Life span: males: 5-7 years; females: up to 30 years

Glossary

arachnid (uh-RAK-nid)—a group of animals that includes spiders, scorpions, mites, and ticks

burrow (BUHR-oh)—a hole or tunnel used as a house

contintent (KAHN-tuh-nuhnt)—one of earth's seven large land masses

habitat (HAB-uh-tat)—the natural place and conditions in which a plant or animal lives

mate (MATE)—to join with another to produce young

molt (MOHLT)—to shed an outer layer of skin

predator (PRED-uh-tur)—an animal that hunts other animals for food

prey (PRAY)—an animal hunted by another animal for food

silk (SILK)—a thin but strong thread made by spiders

venom (VEN-uhm)—a poisonous liquid produced by some animals

vibration (vye-BRAY-shuhn)—a fast movement back and forth

Read More

Archer, Claire. *Tarantula Spiders*. Minneapolis: Abdo Kids, 2015.

Dell, Pamela. *Arachnids*. North Mankato, MN: Capstone Press, 2017.

Spanier, Kristine. *Tarantulas*. Minneapolis: Bullfrog Books, 2019.

Internet Sites

Cool Kid Facts – Tarantula Facts
coolkidfacts.com/tarantula-facts/

National Geographic Kids - Tarantulas
kids.nationalgeographic.com/animals/
tarantula/#tarantula-closeup-hand.jpg

San Diego Zoo Kids - Tarantulas
kids.sandiegozoo.org/animals/tarantula

Index